How to Measure the Weather

by Carol Talley

Scott Foresman
is an imprint of

PEARSON

Glenview, Illinois • Boston, Massachusetts • Chandler, Arizona
Upper Saddle River, New Jersey

ISBN 13: 978-0-328-51401-4
ISBN 10: 0-328-51401-2

4 5 6 7 8 9 10 V0FL 14 13 12 11

Thermometer
on a hot day

Temperature is the warmth or coldness
the air. You can feel changes in the air's
perature. Our bodies sweat when we
feeling hot.

Our bodies react to
air temperature.

Air is all around us. Air can be warm [or] cold. It can be dry or full of rain or snow[.] The changes in the air are called weathe[r.] Meteorologists are people who measure these changes. They predict how the weather will change.

A sudden win[d] sends a girl's h[air] flying into the [air.]

We use thermometers to measure air temperature. Temperature is measured in degrees Celsius or degrees Fahrenheit.

On a Celsius thermometer the freezing point is 0 degrees. The freezing point on a Fahrenheit thermometer is 32 degrees.

Thermometer on a cold day

This girl can feel the direction of the wind.

Wind, or moving air, is a part of weather. You can't see the wind. But you can feel which way it is moving. Strong storm winds can affect the ocean's tides and cause huge waves to erupt.

A wind is named for the direction it is coming from. A north wind is coming from the north.

A weather vane swings around in moving air. Its arrow end points in the direction the wind is coming from.

Weather vane

Which direction is the wind coming from?

Snow blows off the Matterhorn in Switzerland.

Wind speed is measured in miles per hour. Chimney smoke rises straight up in wind that blows less than one mile an hour. You can outrun that wind easily! But winds on a mountain peak are much stronger!

An anemometer is one instrument that measures wind speed. The cups on an anemometer spin when they catch the wind. The anemometer measures the speed of the spinning cups.

A scientist uses an anemometer in Antarctica.

The San Francisco skyline is partly covered with fog.

The air is never totally dry, even in deserts. There is always some water in the air. You can see water in the misty air near waterfalls. You can see it in a foggy harbor. You see water when it rains or snows.

Rain and snow are measured in inches. You can measure rain with a rain gauge. You can measure snow with a ruler or yardstick.

You can make a rain gauge. Put a tin can in an open place. After a rainstorm, use a ruler to measure the depth of the water in the can. You could do this for a whole year. Then you could divide the inches for the year by twelve to get a monthly average.

Students measure and record rainfall using a rain gauge.

A barometer
measures air
pressure.

Air pressure is the weight of the air that presses down on Earth. As air pressure changes, the weather changes. We measure air pressure with a barometer.

Thermometers, weather vanes, anemometers, rain gauges, yardsticks, and barometers all measure weather!